Greg Coope

Melodic Lines

for the Intermediate Guitarist

For those interested in expanding melodic concepts

Divided in eight specific chapters: 1. Picking Exercises, 2. Major Lines,
3. Minor Lines, 4. Minor Pentatonic, 5. Dominant Lines, 6. Altered Lines,
7. Blues Turn-arounds, 8. Jazz Turn-arounds.

Cover Art - Kristi Jorgensen
Cover Layout - Shawn Brown
Music Notation - George Ports
Inside Illustrations - James Koukos
Editor - Dore Rabinoff
Production - Nirvana Alonso

ISBN 1-57424-109-5
SAN 683-8022

Acknowledgements

THANKS TO...

My parents, Bette and Jim

My wife Dore, for bringing it home

My students, Katsumi, Carole, Frank, Joel, Zach, Keith, Jim, Tim, Marty and Ray

Ron Middlebrook of Centerstream Publications

Jim Day - Pacifica, CA

Doug Rogers of MuseEdit Software (www.musedit.com)

Brad Wendkos at True Fire (www.truefire.com)

Ron Veil at Uncle Spot (www.unclespot.com)

Phil and Judy Emerson at Phil's Guitar (www.philsguitars.com)

Rendall Wall & Bill Paige at Heritage Guitar

Harp player extraordinaire, James Faifua of "The Jukes"

_____

In Rememberance
Danny Gatton
"The Humbler"
Sept. 4, 1945 - Oct. 20, 1994

_____

Contents and CD Track List

Rhythm Guitar on RIGHT channel, Melodic Line on LEFT Channel

Foreword...

This book is intended for the intermediate guitarist who is interested in expanding their melodic concepts.

Most of these ideas were realized during my 25 years as a professional teacher and musician. Some of them were borrowed from my guitar idols, some, inspired during the writing of this book.

I have divided the book into eight specific chapters. They are:

1. Picking Exercises:
Here are some picking exercises that you can use to warm up. You should use a metronome and play these slowly and evenly, eventually building up speed and articulation. Employ up picking, down picking and alternate picking on each example.

2. Major Lines:
These lines can be played exclusively in a major key (for example, key of C Major), or over a minor chord a minor third below (A Minor). Some of these lines have passing tones that create interest for the player and listener, making the line less "scaley" and

3. Minor Lines:
These lines can be played exclusively in a minor situation (A Minor) or a minor third above (C Major). Once again, tones outside the minor scale are used in some examples.

4. Minor Pentatonic:
One of the first things aspiring lead guitarists learn. Also known as the "blues scale", the minor pentatonic is a five note scale.

5. Dominant Lines:
These lines can also be used in the blues context as well as jazz. They can be played over dominant chords, in this case: C7, C9, or C13

6. Altered Lines:
Generally used in Jazz, altered lines and chords are a member of the dominant family. Chords with one or more of the following tones: $^b5, ^\#5, ^b9, ^\#9, ^b13$, would be considered altered chords. For example C7$^\#9$, C7$^b9$, C7$^\#9$ $^\#5$, C7$^b9$ $^b5$, etc.

7. Blues Turnarounds:
Here are some lines you can play over the V and IV chord (in this case G7 and F7) in a blues turnaround. A common example of a blues turnaround is the last four measures of a 12 measure blues.

8. Jazz Turnarounds:
I've labeled this chapter "Jazz Turnarounds" even though it is commonly known as ii-V-I (two, five, one) changes. A cornerstone in Jazz tunes it is often employed for setting up key changes within a tune. There are many approaches to playing over the V chord. Altered scales are one way to add "tension and dimension".

Presented are four or five melodic lines on each page. Each line is notated in standard notation and tablature. A neck block on the preceding page demonstrates a suggested position for the line.

You'll find the "essence" of the line within the first 2 or three bars. The last bar or two contains the chord the line may be played over. Most examples are in the key of C and I've purposely kept the rhythms simple (eighth notes).

Do not be deceived by the "thickness" of this book. There is plenty of material here. It has kept some of my most advanced students busy for months, especially when each line is transposed to all 12 keys.

The Developing musician should not merely copy these line, but embellish them, creating melodic lines of their own.

Keep on Pluckin'
Greg Cooper

EXPLANATION OF NECK BLOCKS

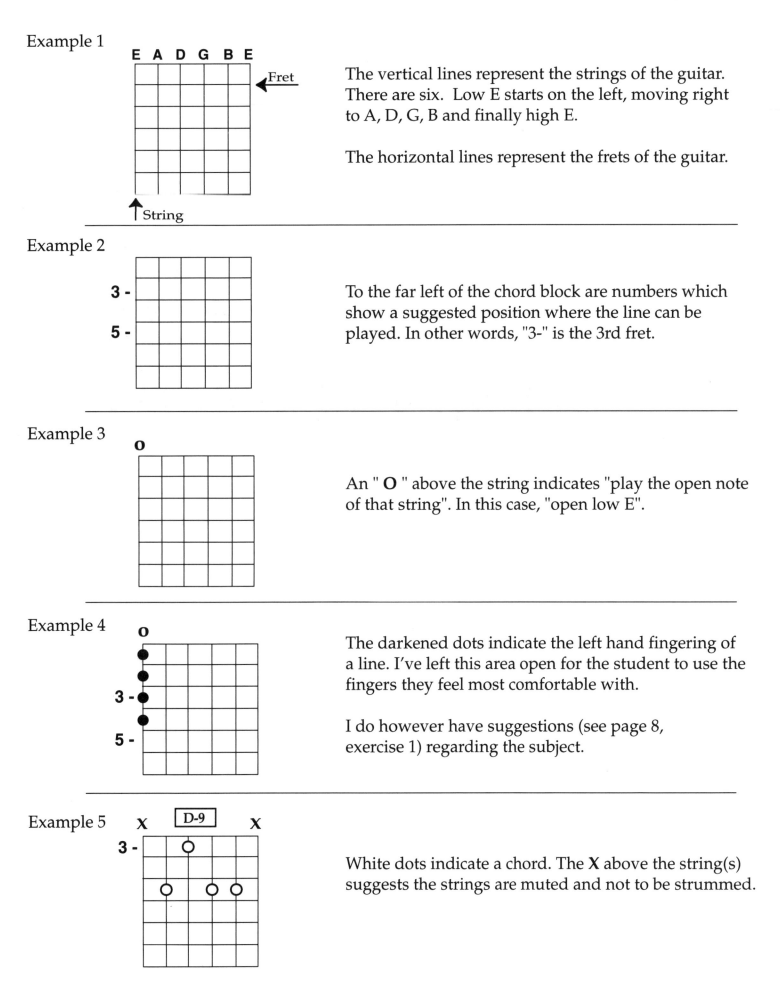

Example 1

The vertical lines represent the strings of the guitar. There are six. Low E starts on the left, moving right to A, D, G, B and finally high E.

The horizontal lines represent the frets of the guitar.

Example 2

To the far left of the chord block are numbers which show a suggested position where the line can be played. In other words, "3-" is the 3rd fret.

Example 3

An " O " above the string indicates "play the open note of that string". In this case, "open low E".

Example 4

The darkened dots indicate the left hand fingering of a line. I've left this area open for the student to use the fingers they feel most comfortable with.

I do however have suggestions (see page 8, exercise 1) regarding the subject.

Example 5

White dots indicate a chord. The **X** above the string(s) suggests the strings are muted and not to be strummed.

PICKING EXERCISES

PICKING EXERCISES

Here are some picking exercises that you can use to warm up. You should use a metronome and play these slowly and evenly, eventually building up speed and articulation. Employ up picking, down picking and alternate picking on each example.

Exercise 1 is a chromatic scale starting on the low E string.

Left hand order:
-Open string
-Index
-Middle
-Ring
-Pinky

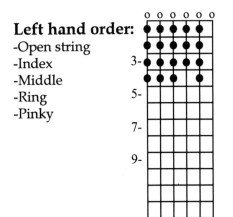

In **Exercise 2**, think of a guitar with an endless number of strings, then alternate pick a major 7th arpeggio pattern.

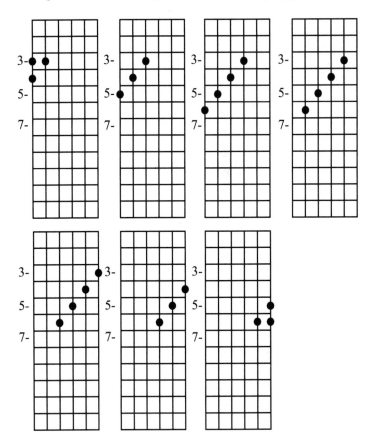

Exercise 3 is a three octave chromatic run starting on first fret F. Use the suggested fingering below and repeat chromatically until index finger is on the 13th fret F (low E string).

Left Hand Use:
-Index on E string
-Middle finger on D string
-Pinky finger on B string

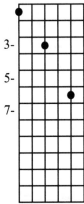

PICKING EXERCISES

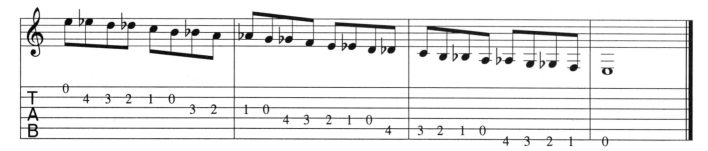

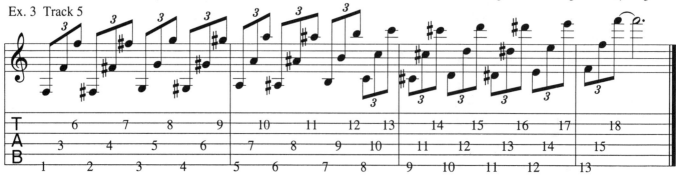

MAJOR LINES

MAJOR LINES

These lines can be played exclusively in a major key (for example, key of C Major), or over a minor chord a minor third below (A Minor). Some of these lines have passing tones that create interest for the player and listener, making the line less "scaley" and predictable.

Line 1 starts on the major 7th (B) and moves a half step to the root. Think 7th, root, 3rd, 5th. This line moves from 3rd position (A) string and ends up around the 7th position (E and B) strings.

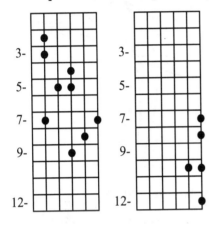

Line 2 is a C major scale in the 7th position with alternating 2nd's.

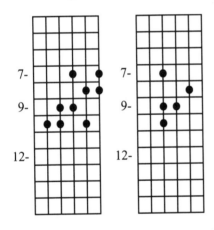

Line 3 is played on the (D, G & B) strings. It has passing tones (Eb, Gb) played on the (B) string if started in the 5th position and ending up on the 9th fret E (G string).

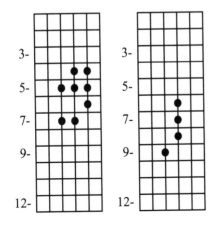

Line 4 has a "falling down steps" feel. Lots of chromatic passing tones. Moves from 7th position, ending on 2nd fret E (D string).

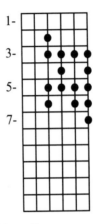

Line 5 basically consists of four notes in three octaves. Starting at 7th position B (low E string), and ending up at the 15th fret G (high E string).

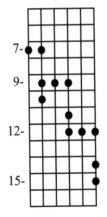

MAJOR LINES

Line 1 Track 6

Line 2 Track 7

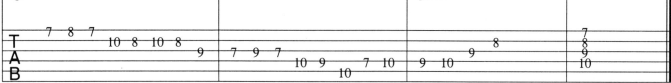

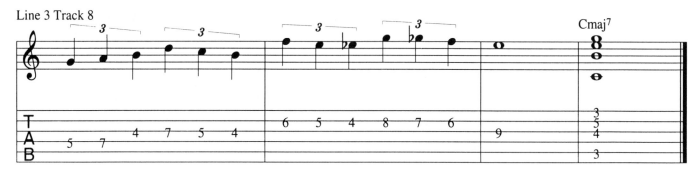

Line 3 Track 8

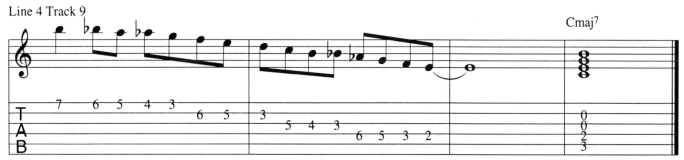

Line 4 Track 9

Line 4 Track 10

MORE MAJOR LINES

Line 1 is just a C major scale, starting on the root tone and ending on a 5th. What's interesting about it, is it moves down the neck as it moves up in pitch.

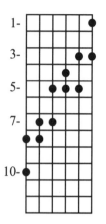

Line 2 employs four arpeggios. All are contained within a C major scale. E minor (♭7, 5, ♭3, root), B diminished (♭7, ♭5, ♭3, root), A minor (♭7, 5, ♭3, root) and E minor again (♭7, 5, ♭3, root).

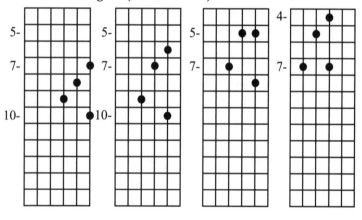

Line 3 is in the key of E major. Take note that in the middle of bar 1, a B dominant 7 arpeggio connects the E (1,3,5) to a relative minor (C# minor) run.

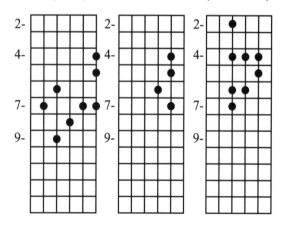

For **line 4**, we are back in the key of C with a line that uses passing tones chromatically, to give a "climbing" effect.

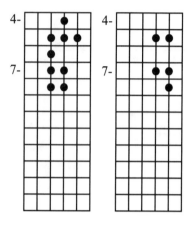

Not much to analyze in **line 5**, just a catchy little phrase I borrowed from a Tal Farlow solo.

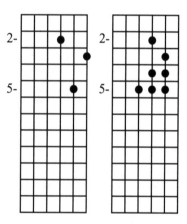

MORE MAJOR LINES

Line 1 Track 11

Line 2 Track 12

Line 3 Track 13

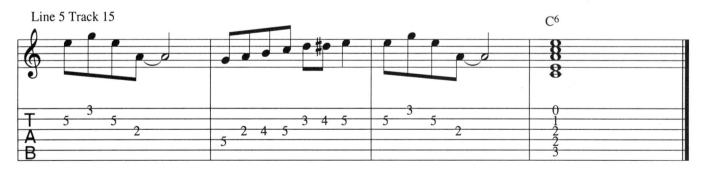

Line 4 Track 14

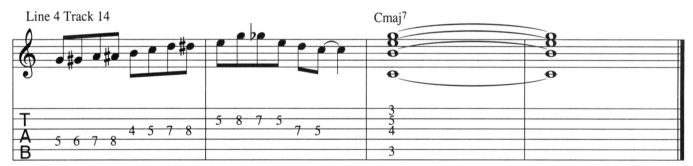

Line 5 Track 15

MORE MAJOR LINES - Key of G

Line 1 starts with an E minor 7th arpeggio on the A, D, B and G strings (5th to 9th position). It also employs blue notes ♭3 and ♭5 as the line descends.

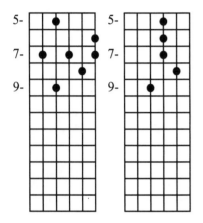

Line 2 is an idea realized from a Jimmy Raney run. The ♭5 or #11 gives it a *lydian* sound, but it can also be used with a regular major 7th.

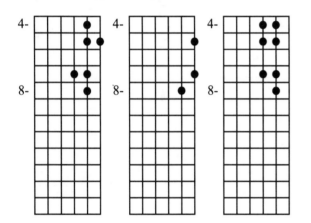

Line 3 works best in the *lydian* (#11) mode. Starting on the Major 7th (F#) on the low E string and ending on a 9th (A) on the high E string.

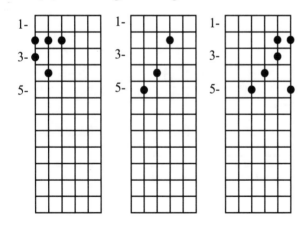

Line 4 is a Paganini type run, reminiscent of Eric Johnson. It is straight major with alternating thirds.

Starting on the 12th fret E and ending on G on the low E string, it covers alot of territory. I like this line because it moves in whole steps.

A power chord that is all root tones and 5ths really brings this riff home (ala E.J.).

G Power Chord

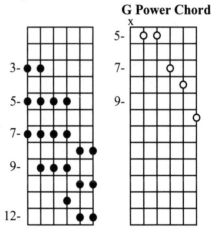

MORE MAJOR LINES - Key of G

Line 1 Track 16

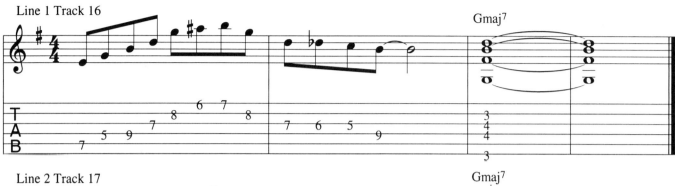

Line 2 Track 17

Line 3 Track 18

Line 4 Track 19

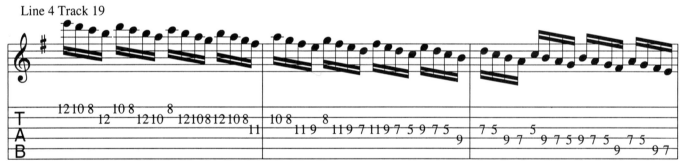

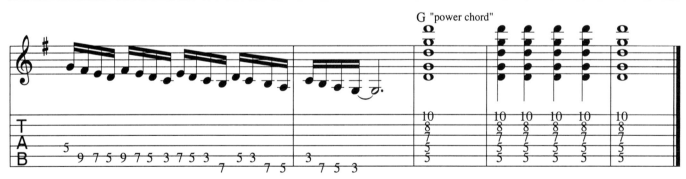

15

MINOR LINES

MINOR LINES

These lines can be played exclusively in a minor situation (A Minor) or a minor third above (C Major). Once again, tones outside the minor scale are used in some examples.

Line 1 is really two arpeggios; an A minor 7th and an E minor. Start with your middle finger on fret 5 of the low E. This minor 9th arpeggio sweeps all six strings from the 3rd to 7th frets.

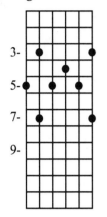

The first measure in **Line 2** is an ascending minor 9th arpeggio, starting on the D string in the 7th position. It descends diatonically, incorporating a major 3rd (C#) on the 6th fret (G string).

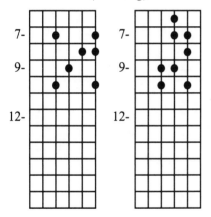

Line 3 uses a chromatic passage (F#, G, G#) on the G string, then repeats up an octave between the 12th and 15th frets of the high E string.

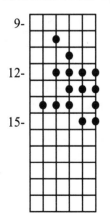

Line 4 is a minor line with a major 7th (G#).

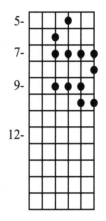

Line 5 is a "Wes style" line with b9 (Bb) and b5 (Eb) passing tones. Slur b9 (Bb) to 9th (B) at beginning of phrase.

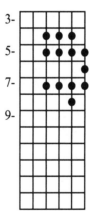

MINOR LINES

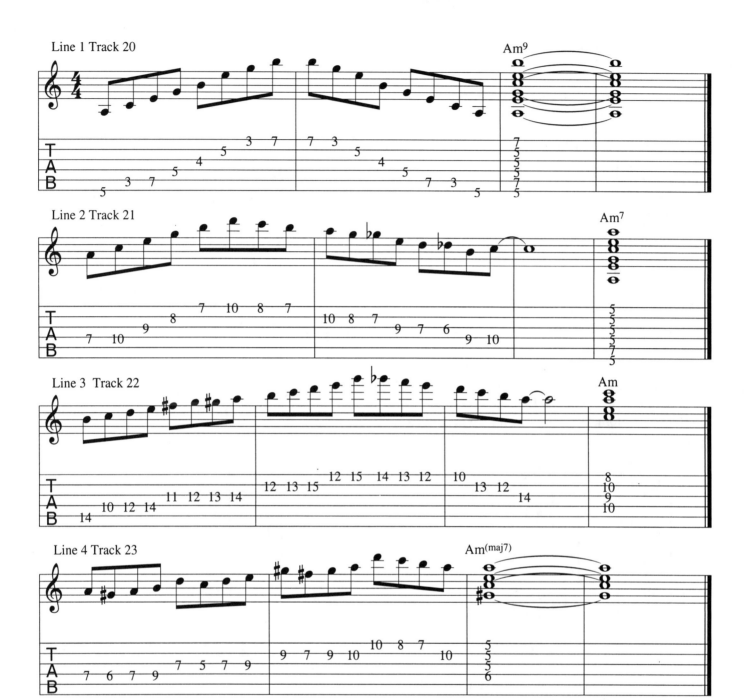

MORE MINOR LINES

Line 1 utilizes a chromatic passage that repeats an octave higher (9th, 11th, 3rd, *b*3rd).

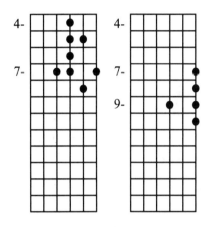

Bar 1 of **Line 2** is a diatonic D Minor scale, starting on a 2nd and ending on a 9th.

In Bar 2, a major 7th is employed.

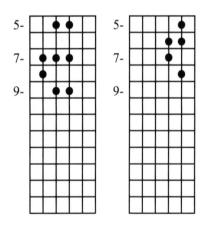

Line 3 starts with a diminished arpeggio in B. It also contains a major 7th tone (G#).

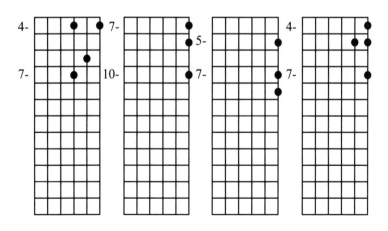

Once again, **line 4** employs the major 7th tone in a minor context.

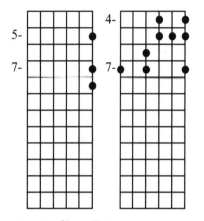

Finally, **line 5** alternates minor chords with diminished chords. Notice the notes on the high E string move diatonically up the G minor scale. Django and Wes Montgomery were two guitarists who often incorporated this technique within their solos.

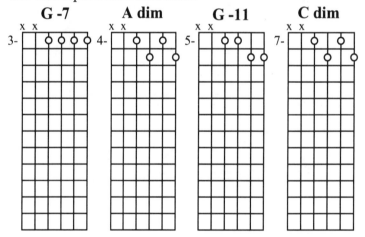

MORE MINOR LINES

Line 1 Track 25

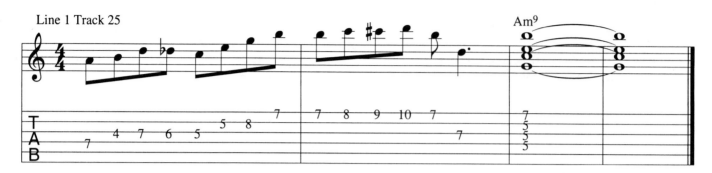

Line 2 Track 26

Line 3 Track 27

Line 4 Track 28

Line 5 Track 29

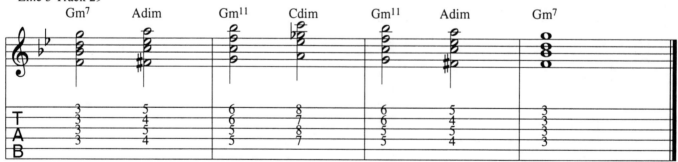

MINOR PENTATONIC

MINOR PENTATONIC

One of the first things aspiring lead guitarists learn. Also known as the "blues scale", the minor pentatonic is a five note scale.

3 Octave A minor

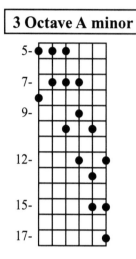

Line 1 is an alternate 4th's and 5th's pattern that can be played in 2nd position

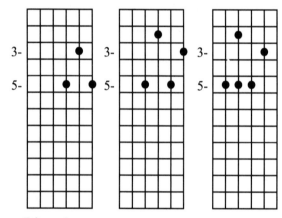

Line 2 is a "Jimmy Vaughan" style lick.

In the second set of quarter note triplets, play the first A on the 5th fret E string. Slide the second A to the 10th fret B string from the 8th fret.

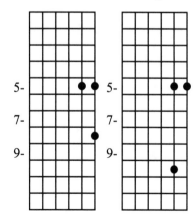

Line 3 is simply an A minor pentatonic with a b5 (Eb) passing tone. You would be surprised at the number of intermediate students that haven't discovered this.

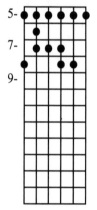

Line 4 covers alot of vertical territory. Starting in 12th position moving through 9th, 5th and 3rd positions, to include an open 6th string E in the second set of eighth note triplets.

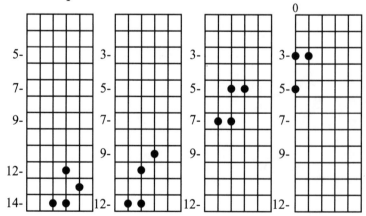

MINOR PENTATONIC

Am pentatonic scale Track 30

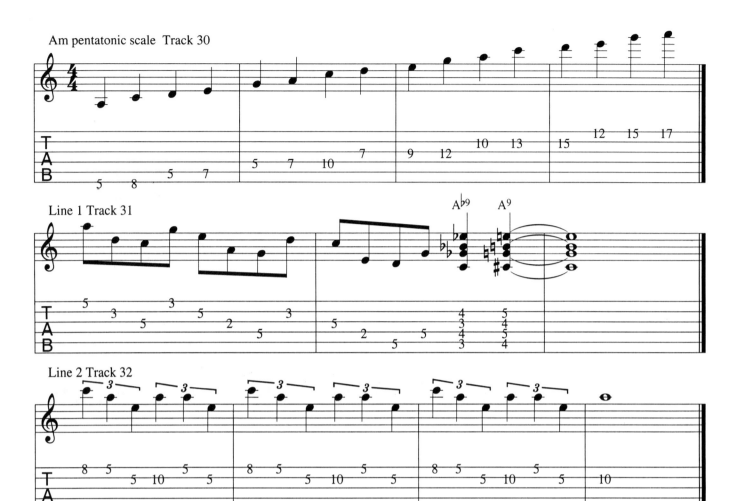

Line 1 Track 31

Line 2 Track 32

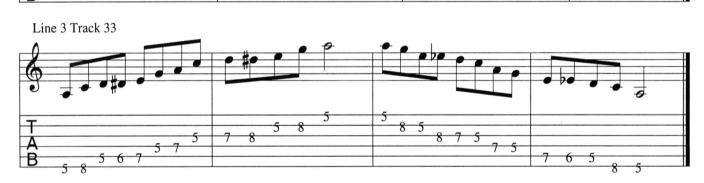

Line 3 Track 33

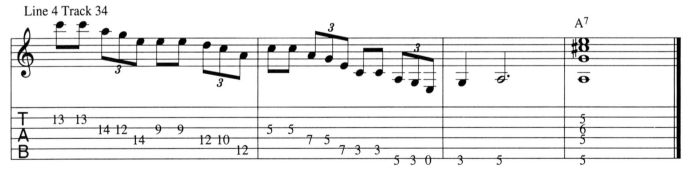

Line 4 Track 34

DOMINANT LINES

DOMINANT LINES

These lines can also be used in the blues context as well as jazz. They can be played over dominant chords, in this case: C7, C9, or C13

Line 1 can be played between the 1st and 5th position using "blue notes" (b2, b5) as passing tones.

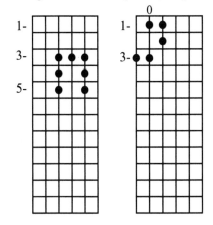

When **line 2** is analyzed, it reveals a C7 arpeggio and a D minor 7th arpeggio that fits well over C13.

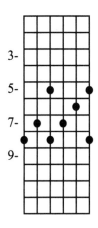

Line 3 alternates between the root (C) and 5 (G), b5 (Gb), 4 (F) and major 3rd (E). Then repeat down an octave.

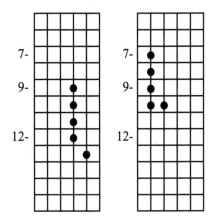

When **line 4** is analyzed, it reveals four arpeggios.

D minor 7th in 5th position
C minor 7th in 3rd position
G minor 7th in 3rd position
D minor 7th in 2nd position

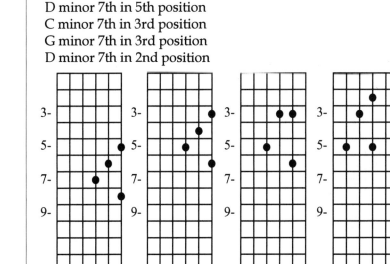

Line 5 lays well around the 10th fret. Think D natural minor scale or C mixolydian.

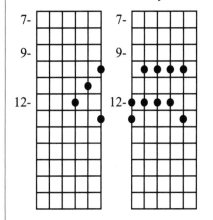

DOMINANT LINES

Line 1 Track 35

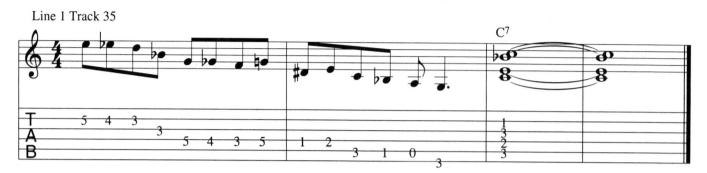

Line 2 Track 36

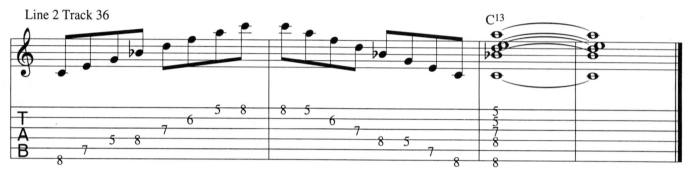

Line 3 Track 37

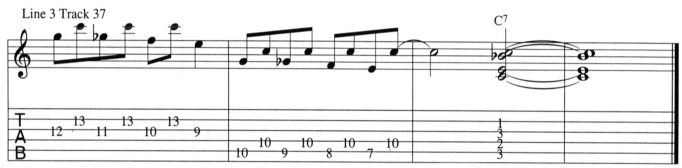

Line 4 Track 38

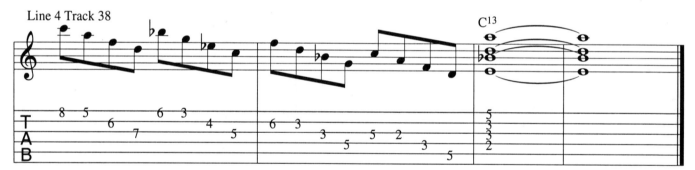

Line 5 Track 39

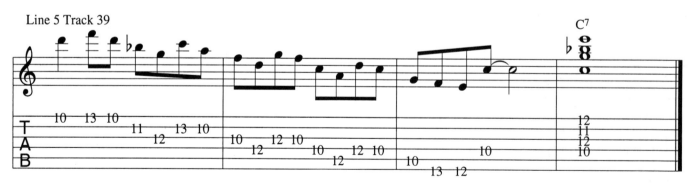

MORE DOMINANT LINES

Line 1 is a descending mixolydian scale using a *b*3 (E*b*) blue note.

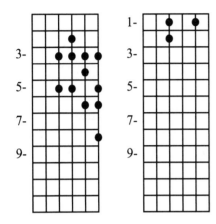

Line 2 is a box pattern around the 3rd and 5th frets of the top four strings (D, G, B, E). Blue notes *b*3 (E*b*) and *b*5 (G*b*) are used.

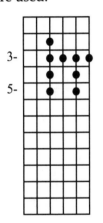

Line 3 is a hybrid scale using blue notes *b*3 (E*b*), *b*5 (G*b*), as well as a #5 (A*b*) passing tone. This line could be applied to C altered chords (C7#5, C7*b*5) also.

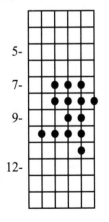

Line 4 is a G harmonic minor pattern applied to a C dominant chord. Thinking **up** a fifth in a minor key is a good way to add color to dominant lines.

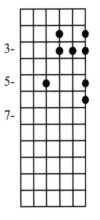

If **line 5** seems familiar...it is (*Major lines, line 1*). This major 7th arpeggio (B*b*) works wll over C dominant.

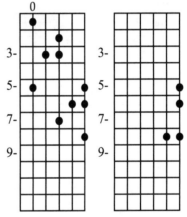

MORE DOMINANT LINES

Line 1 Track 40

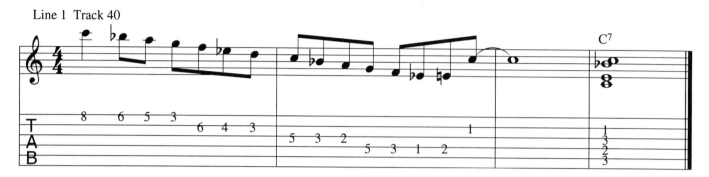

Line 2 Track 41

Line 3 Track 42

Line 4 Track 43

Line 4 Track 44

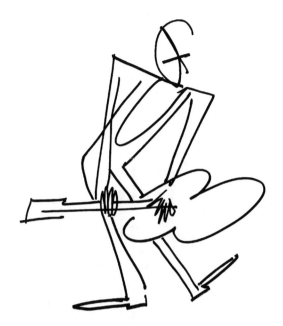

ALTERED LINES

ALTERED LINES

Generally used in Jazz, altered lines and chords are a member of the dominant family. Chords with one or more of the following tones: ♭5, ♯5, ♭9, ♯9, ♭13, would be considered altered chords. For example C7♭9, C7♯9, C7♭9♯5, C7♯9♯5, etc.

Line 1 is a diminished pattern: 1, ♭3, ♭2 (E♭, G♭, E♭9) moving down the neck in intervals of 6th's.

Line 4 works well in 8th position and incorporates the following tones; ♭3, ♭9, #5, ♭7 (E♭, D♭, A♭, B♭).

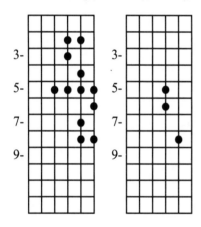

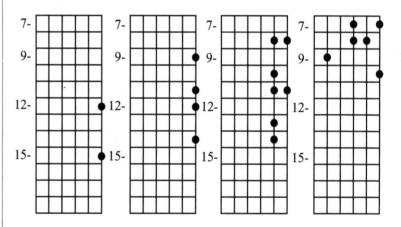

Line 2 starts with the mixolydian scale and gets a little "outside" on the third beat; ♭9, ♭5 (D♭, G♭). Take note of the minor and major 3rd's.

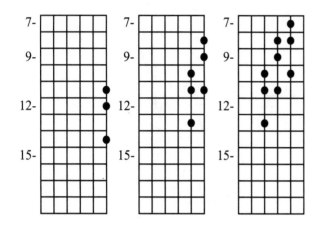
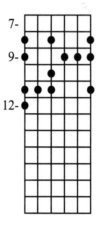

Line 5 is a root-diminished 3rd pattern moving in half-whole steps down the neck.

Line 3 is a half-whole diminished scale pattern; (♭3, ♭5, ♭7, ♭9).

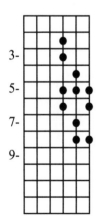

ALTERED LINES

Line 1 Track 45

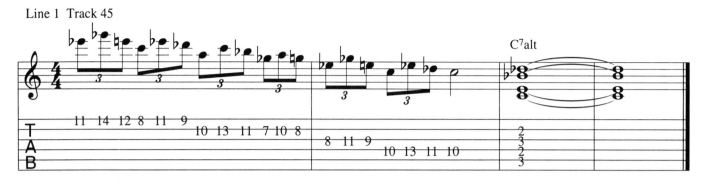

Line 2 Track 46

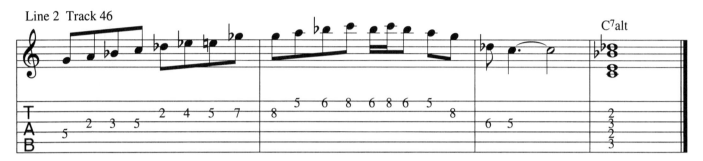

Line 3 Track 47

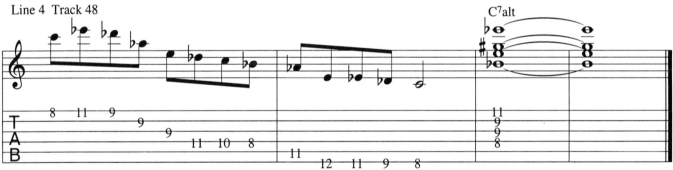

Line 4 Track 48

Line 5 Track 49

BLUES TURN-AROUNDS

BLUES TURNAROUNDS

This page doesn't need a whole lot of individual explanation. The first chord block in each example is the suggested position for the **V** chord line. The second chord block covers the **IV** chord. You'll notice this is usually the same "pattern" down a whole step (2 frets). Occasionally there is a third chord block for the **I** chord line. The neck block for line 5 indicates the position for just the **V** chord. Transpose down a whole step for the **IV** chord.

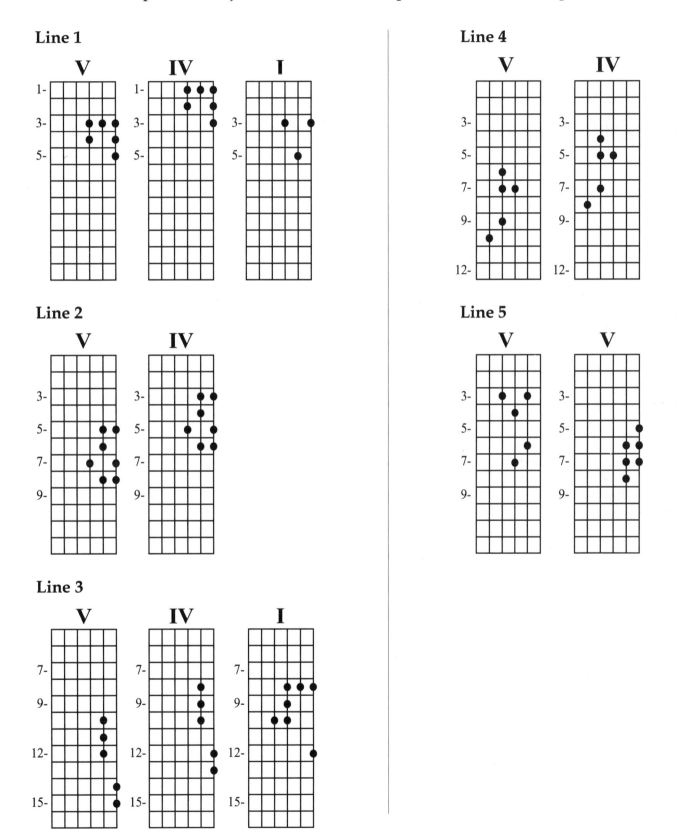

BLUES TURN-AROUNDS (V-IV-I)

Line 1 Track 50

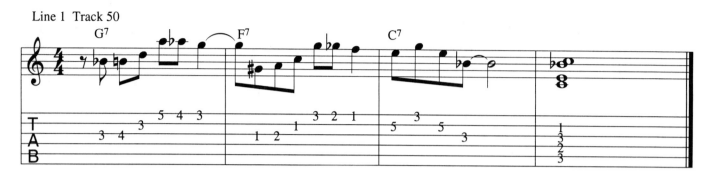

Line 2 Track 51

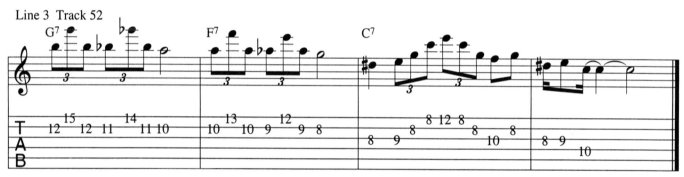

Line 3 Track 52

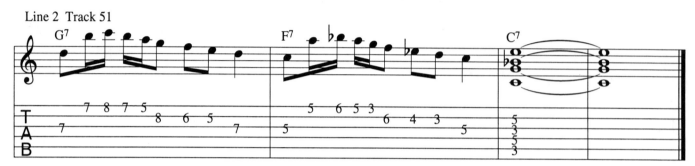

Line 4 Track 53

Line 5 Track 54

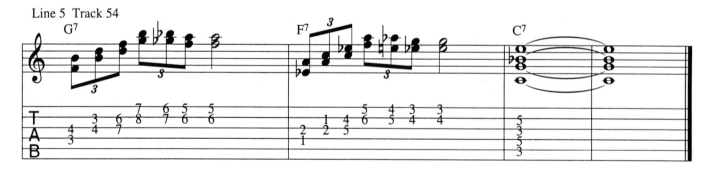

JAZZ TURNAROUNDS

JAZZ TURNAROUNDS

Notice there are alot of altered tones over the **V** chord (*b*9, #9, *b*5, #5). These can be viewed as passing or "*tension*" tones. Once again I've omitted the **I** chord from being voiced on the neck block page, but there is an interesting voicing of the **I** chord in Line 3 (3rd, 7th, root, 5th).

Line 1

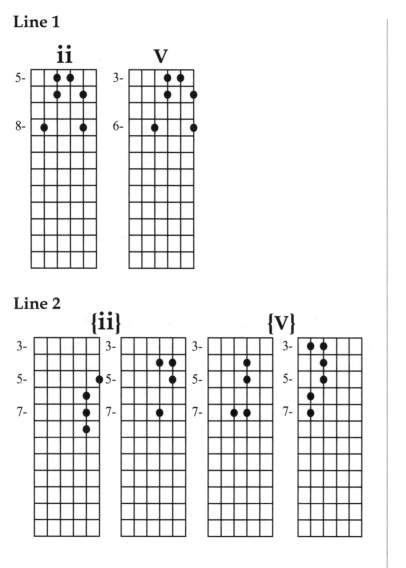

Line 4

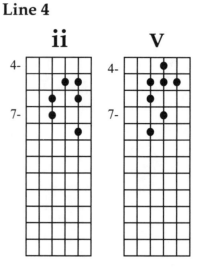

Line 2

Line 5

Line 3

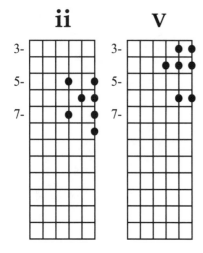

JAZZ TURN-AROUNDS (II-V-I)

Line 1 Track 55

Line 2 Track 56

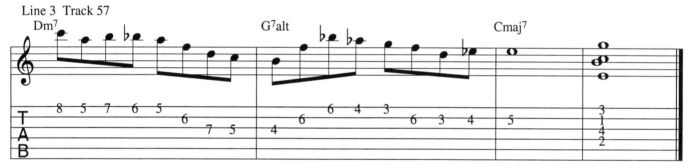

Line 3 Track 57

Line 4 Track 58

Line 5 Track 59

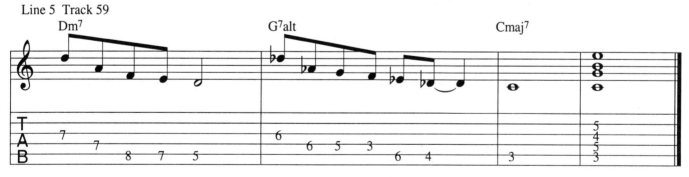

37

About the author...

Teacher at the 2002 National Guitar Workshop in Los Angeles.
As a teacher for 25 years, Greg Cooper has instructed at:

Woodlowe Music - Woodland Hills, CA
Reseda Music - Reseda, CA
Kaye's Music Scene - Reseda, CA
Serramonte Music Center - Daly City, CA
Music Village - Portland, OR

As a student he has studied with some of the worlds most
respected players and teachers:

Phil Upchurch
Ron Anthony
Jimmy Wyble
Jerry Hahn
Charlie Shoemake
Supplemental music studies at Los Angeles Valley College

He has had lessons published in:

Guitar Player Magazine "Sessions" (Aug '99)
Guitar Player Magazine "Lick of the Month" (Nov '98)

Currently, he teaches intermediate to advanced students,
privately from his studio in San Francisco, CA.